"I love my bees"

a novice beekeeper's first year

"I Love My Bees"

© Fiona van Dokkum

ISBN 978-1-904846-64-2

Published by Northern Bee Books, 2010
Scout Bottom Farm
Mytholmroyd
Hebden Bridge HX7 5JS (UK)

Printed by Lightning Source UK

"I love my bees"

a novice beekeeper's first year

NORTHERN BEE BOOKS

To my husband whom I adore, I thank you for your love,
your encouragement and your patience. I know this journey would
not have been possible without you.

And to my father, who would have understood all of it.

Introduction

Anyone who keeps bees knows that bees reflect their mood in the sound they make. When they're calm, they make a calm sound, a soft and soothing hum; when they're excited, they make an excited sound, a more strident buzz. And when they panic, they scream.

I had spent many long minutes watching my bees that afternoon, sitting in my chair next to the hive. They were coming and going as usual, intent on their own business. Finally I got up to leave. Unfortunately I stood up directly into the flight path of a returning forager. She flew straight into my hair.

A bee has a hook on the end of each foot and they very quickly get snagged. The books don't tell you to avoid fluffy jerseys when you visit your apiary, but you should. And you should tie up your hair as well. I learned this one the hard way.

This bee was trapped, somewhere just above my right ear. She couldn't get out and her buzz went up a few notches. Shaking my head wasn't enough to dislodge her so I bent double, let my hair hang down to the ground, and shook again. Still not enough. I knew I was going to get stung. There was no possible chance I wouldn't. It was just a matter of time... I started running my fingers through my hair, quickly, over and over. The buzzing became a shrill siren of desperation. I'm going to get stung! I'm going to get stung! I'm going to get stung! I was almost singing it to myself as I flicked my fingers through my hair, and flicked and flicked, unable to escape this piercing wail of panic against my scalp.

Suddenly I heard her fall. She landed in the grass two feet from me, rested for a moment, tested her wings, and flew home.

I straightened up, breathless in the silence.

Glossary

There are many very good books about beekeeping practices which are available on the open market. This does not pretend to be one of them. This is simply my journal of my first beekeeping year. There is much that isn't explained which may confuse a complete outsider, so in order to provide a small amount of clarification, I set out below a glossary of certain beekeeping terms that I have used – explained as I understand them (and not to be confused with a definitive interpretation).

Brood refers to baby bees. 'Unsealed brood' refers to open cells in which eggs or larvae can be seen. 'Sealed brood' applies to larvae which have been covered over by the bees (slightly raised coverings for workers, humped for drones, thimble-shaped for potential queens).

The term **drawing out** (alternatively referred to as 'drawing down') comb applies to the cell-building work that bees do on a brand new sheet of foundation wax (so called because it gives the bees a foundation on which to build). I didn't know in the early days that foundation wax comes in different grades – I only learned later to ask for 'premier' foundation from my supplier – apparently bees prefer the higher grade wax. To be honest, I haven't noticed any difference between them. If the bees have work to do they'll do it, no matter what you give them!

The word **'super'** refers to the smaller box of a standard hive which usually sits on top of the brood chamber. There are many different designs of hive available. I use a National hive. I would like to use a WBC – the more traditional type of hive – but I can't afford one. Generally, a super is used as a honey store and the queen is confined to the brood chamber, where she lays and where the baby bees are born.

The term **'crown board'**, which I have used frequently, refers to a square sheet of wood with (usually) two round-ended oblong holes which rests on top of the hive chambers, underneath the roof or lid.

Fondant is bakers' fondant, a sort of solid icing sugar.

Nuc (short for nucleus) **boxes** are smaller hive boxes in which half the usual number of frames can be held. These are ideal for housing small colonies of bees which don't need as much space as an entire hive.

Propolis is bee glue, gathered from the resin of trees and plants. Bees use it to stick things together, seal gaps if there are drafts and generally protect the hive from the elements.

I have found that my bees use very little propolis – I have never had to use a hive tool to move or remove parts of my hives – and I have a sneaking suspicion that it may have something to do with smoke; the more they are smoked, the more the bees will use propolis. I do not know this for a fact, but it's an attractive theory. Certainly all the hive openings I have attended elsewhere where smoke has been used liberally have been very sticky affairs indeed.

The term 'robbing' refers to bees invading a neighbouring hive in order to steal their honey. I have wondered whether the urge for the bees to do this has anything to do with lack of forage. In places where large numbers of hives are kept, strain is put on local resources and bees may find themselves competing for nectar. How much easier, then, to steal from your neighbour.

And finally, right at the end of this book I have referred to my bees as 'children-of-the-sun'. This term will no doubt confuse anybody who has not read the lectures given by the German philosopher Rudolph Steiner. He spoke at length about bees' connection with the sun, the 21-day cycle in which the sun revolves on its own axis, and the connection between this cycle and the time it takes for bees to go from egg to hatching. Queen bees, he stated, are entirely dominated by the sun, having been laid and born within the sun's 21-day cycle. Worker bees are also wholly influenced, he asserted, because their development within the cell coincides exactly with the cycle of the sun. Whether I believe Steiner's assertions or not, since I read his book I have thought of my worker bees as 'children-of-the-sun'.

A photograph of my first hive

I collected my bees from a local beekeeper and put the sealed hive in the back of my car. I drove away, excited but very nervous. No more than fifty yards down the lane I noticed two bees flying around in the back window – inside the car! Oh no! Now what? I drove a little further and suddenly there were lots of bees in the back window. Oh help! I pulled off the road and opened the boot of my car. There were bees everywhere. Eeeeek! I lifted the hive out of the car and put it on the ground, desperately trying to find the hole they were getting out of. Almost immediately I got stung on the very front of my throat. Lesson one: Put the suit on *before* you handle the bees.

There I was, on the side of the road, feeling rather obvious in my beesuit, bees everywhere, wondering how on earth I was going to stop them all flying away. And trying not to panic and run. I phoned for help.

Bee friends raced to my rescue from both directions, the box was properly sealed with tape (my own fault – when building the floor I hadn't used enough drawing pins to hold the mesh in place) and returned to the boot of my car. I was assured that, despite the bees flying around inside my car, they should stay in the windows and I would be fine for the journey home. Of course, I couldn't drive in my beesuit…

One bee kept me company the entire trip on the armrest of my door, right next to my right elbow. The others stayed in the windows as I'd been promised.

We got home safely and I had survived my baptism of fire.

My Journal begins ....

14.8.09

I collected my bees today! One frame of eggs, three frames of brood. So. A laying queen plus brood (baby bees) plus room for stores.

Instructions: Feed them syrup (water plus sugar, 2 to 1).

16.8.09

The hive is quiet, the bees busy. Lots of to-ing and fro-ing. Pollen is being collected (pollen colours yellow and orange).

17.8.09

p.m. The hive is noisy! Lots of activity, 2 dozen plus flying around outside the hive. Lots of fanning. Was yesterday quiet and today normal? I don't know yet!

I added some camomile tea and a tiny amount of salt to the syrup in accordance with biodynamic beliefs (that it makes it easier for the bees to convert the syrup into honey for storage). The bees make straight for the syrup – even sitting on my gloved fingers with their tongues out.

I wonder if a storm is coming. I stand a little way off and watch them.
Ouch! One made straight for my face and stung my upper lip.

Lesson 1: Don't get too close when they're antsy.
Lesson 2: Don't swat at bees or try to brush them off, they sting.
Lesson learned.
No storm.

18.8.09

3.30 p.m. Again, very busy, lots of activity.

20.8.09

I checked the syrup today, around 4.30 p.m. Bees really quiet. I even lifted the bucket to weigh it and they barely moved! Still pollen collecting, of course, coming and going.

Intermittent heavy showers / sun. They're definitely collecting the syrup but not making much headway with the +/- two litres I gave them.

23.8.09

I checked on my bees this afternoon, five-ish. Two dead bees outside the hive. Two more are moving unnaturally on the ground. Should I be worried?

(Put mite board under the hive today to do a 24hr varroa check.)

Read my beekeeping books – most obvious possibility for dead and/or agitated bees: wasps. I've seen two nearby, more than once. Will watch carefully.

Further observation: (1) Definitely a different buzz in the hive; (2) The bees are very agitated and checking each other carefully; and (3) one wasp very much in evidence, trying to get in, even walking on the bottom (mesh floor) of the hive. Hope I see a dead one tomorrow. (I have always hated wasps but now I feel protective of my bees and am doubly vigilant).

I spent some time sitting really close to the hive entrance. Even in their agitated state the bees accepted my presence. I suspect they may have been more focused on the wasp.

My hive came supplied with a bright yellow plastic square which fits on runners underneath the mesh hive floor. By inserting this and leaving it in place for 24 hours, I can examine the hive debris which falls through the mesh and check for varroa. At first, a magnifying glass helped because I didn't really know what I was looking for. Also, using a damp finger to pick the mites up and then dropping them into an eggcup of water makes it much easier to get an accurate count when they've all been collected.

25.8.09

10 a.m. I watched bees emerging from the hive to greet the new day. Early risers already returning with pollen.

p.m. Saw a wasp on the hive! Dispatched it with my hand. It landed on the slate landing board and one bee immediately dragged it off the edge. Guards understandably agitated.

Later p.m. Another wasp! Right near to the slate. I killed this one too.

Note to self: When you open the hive ---

First check brood / stores
Then dust for mites (with mite board already in place under the hive)
Then check syrup supply.

26.8.09

FIRST HIVE OPENING.

> Gosh, I was nervous! You can read as much as you want but at the end of the day getting up close and personal with your own bees is what it's all about. I double-checked my suit, I pulled on my long-wristed bright yellow kitchen gloves (one size smaller than I would wear for the washing up) and I breathed.   If this went really badly, I would close up and ask for assistance. However, I knew that if it did go badly, I would lose all confidence and probably give the bees back. I had to be able to do this. I took a deep breath.
>
> Standing at the back of the hive – the opposite side to the entrance where the bees are coming and going – I lifted off the lid and laid it top-down on the ground. Then I carefully lifted the crown board and stood that on the ground next to the hive, leaning it against the hive wall. I counted through the frames, naming the first one – the rear most frame nearest to me – as frame number 1.

I made notes as I went:
Frames 1 + 2 – no activity
Frames 3 + 4 – drawing out both sides
Frame 5 – one side half a frame of honey stores!
Frame 6 – top corners both sides of the frame are stores. Almost no brood.
Frame 7 – stores and brood – I saw eggs!
Frame 8 – stores and brood – bigger eggs (now larvae)

Dear God, the wasps!! No sooner had I opened the hive than two appeared, intent on getting in! I managed to kill them without upsetting the bees. I still don't know quite how I did it. Once they were dispatched I replaced the crown board and managed to close up without any further problems.

Checking on the bees later in the afternoon, two more wasps were about and the bees were in a state of some excitement. I despatched two wasps – but no sooner done than another one appeared! In desperation, I put out a jam pot – dollop of jam, quarter-full of water, three yards from the hive – but I hold out little hope of distracting the wasps. In all I must have killed at least five or six today.

p.m. Wasps still attacking, particularly from underneath the hive. I put the yellow plastic mite board back under the hive and closed off the gaps with tape. The bees almost instantly calmed down both inside and at the entrance. I suspect the wasps trying to get in so close to the brood was too much for them. Do I need to investigate a solid floor?

Final tally on wasp kills for the day = 10.

I didn't use smoke for my first hive opening. This would be one area in which I would break away from established practice from the very beginning.

Before I got my bees I had spent a long time thinking about this aspect of beekeeping. In the first instance, I had a problem approaching any wild animal with the thing it fears most in the world: the threat of fire. In the second instance, I had attended several hive openings at established beekeepers' premises prior to taking possession of my own bees, and I had observed the proceedings very carefully. In my own mind, on not one occasion had the smoker been used effectively, nor had it calmed the bees in any way. In every instance, I had witnessed bees that were agitated and noisy, and in each case they had tried very hard to sting us and had persisted in following us when we walked away. Whilst I understood the reasoning behind it, I questioned the smoker's use and was determined to find a better way. Whether or not it would work – and continue to work – would be between me and my bees. I kept my options open. If I needed a smoker, I had one, but the success of that first hive opening set the tone for future hive openings and to this day my smoker remains in pristine condition, unused.

What I have used instead is a common-or-garden spray bottle, the kind you might use to spray the roses, filled with water. A few squirts of mist are usually enough to move bees out of the way, and I've found it works best if the water drips onto bees, as if it's raining. Then they very quickly head downwards between the frames. By gently moving the bees, I have almost always been able to close up without squashing them. Of course, bees move about constantly, and even though the scene may be set for a perfect roof replacement, some adventurous bee is bound to wander the wrong way and get trapped. I hate it, but it happens.

27.8.09

I took the hose to the apiary today to wash the patio. Two wasps were buzzing around. I pointed the hose at one and it fell to the ground where I stamped on it with glee. The other wasp, the same thing. Waterlog, fall, squish. Eco-friendly and efficient.

I left the hose nearby.

The bees are <u>really</u> quiet today. (windy)

28.8.09

Today I reduced the size of the hive entrance with tape in the hope of giving the bees a more manageable area to guard. It may work, it may not.

p.m. Bees out and about – they seem <u>much</u> happier.

> Shortly after this, I took a small piece of wood and cut a little archway in it. I then nailed this onto the front of the entrance block. It was a bit of a squish for the bees to get through when they were out in numbers, but it worked so well I left it in place for the entire winter and only removed it in early spring.

I found a honey bee walking in the grass and put her on the landing board. Almost immediately two bees emerged from the hive entrance. One jumped on her and the other grabbed her and literally threw her over the edge! Not <u>my</u> bee, then. Fascinating.

30.8.09

My 24-hour varroa mite check ended this evening. Three round-shelled varroa, three walking red things (what are they?).

(Reply on the 'net tells me the little red ones are pollen mites and nothing to worry about – Phew !!)

31.8.09

I killed four wasps at the hive this morning. Checked on jam jar --- twenty-seven dead wasps!

6.9.09

I checked the hive from underneath with a torch (looking up through the mesh floor). Frames 5 – 9 are <u>heavy</u> with bees.

I had a long chat with an experienced local beekeeper today. He suggested I move frames 11 and 12 (which are empty) to the back of the hive. With the brood nest nearer the entrance, the bees will guard better and they tend to work from front to back in any event.

He also suggested I insulate on top of the crown board with polystyrene to help the bees keep heat in the hive over winter.

He also suggested I leave them alone as much as I can!

9.9.09

I dusted my bees today (the first fine morning for <u>days</u>). I opened the hive with almost no objection from the bees.

I've been watching the hive from below – there's lots of activity on frames 1 and 2. Drawing out comb perhaps?

> The simplest and most biodynamic way of treating bees for varroa mites is to dust them with icing sugar. Ideally, this would be icing sugar without corn starch (which is included in commercially available icing sugar). The idea behind this is that when dusted, the bees, attracted by the sugar, will set to work cleaning each other and in doing so, dislodge any varroa which may be sitting on a bee's back. However, this method **will not** deal with varroa which have already tucked themselves away inside the brood cells. Apparently they particularly favour the cells of drones because these are larger and give the varroa more space in which to breed.

11.9.09

The bees are bringing in <u>four</u> types of pollen now: light yellow, bright yellow, dark orange and greyish.

I found a bee on the ground near the hive and picked it up. Its wings were almost completely cut / torn off.

13.9.09

Hive opening today.

No smoke, no water. My bees are <u>good</u>!

I didn't see the queen, they have room to expand, there are three frames with brood, one with cells ready.

Overall I thought it went really well. The bees were gentle, co-operative and patient with me. They moved around on the comb but entirely without panic.

<u>I saw bees dancing</u> !!! How exciting this was to watch!

I didn't see the queen – I didn't want to spend too long looking, even though the sun was full on the hive and it was very warm.

When I open next time I must move frame 1 to position 12.

14.9.09

When I went to check on my bees, I was surprised to see dozens of bees crowded on the landing board! Lots of milling about, moving in and out. I looked underneath the hive; there are at least 20 bees on the underside. What is going on?

p.m. All quiet again.

15.9.09

Wow! That was educational! Sitting watching my bees – lots of activity, dozens of foragers returning with bright yellow pollen – and I saw one bee stumbling around with damaged wings. I picked her up and let her walk around on my hands for a while, then put her on the landing board. Several bees ignored her, so I assumed she must be one of mine. Suddenly one bee jumped on her and bit her one wing – I could see her mouth parts holding on and tugging at her, the aggressor's body going from side to side. Then the aggressor took off – carrying the other bee – and flew one foot into the grass, literally carrying her away, and pushed her down into the grass and left her there.

Conclusive proof: the wing damage is <u>caused</u>, not a birth defect.

16.9.09

Okay child, time to review the situation. My research tells me wing deformities can be a sign of Deformed Wing Virus – a result of varroa infestation. The bees doing the 'biting' may only have been clearing the diseased bees out of the hive.

I thought about this.

No. The bee's wings were not deformed, they were deliberately torn. I had watched it happen.

HIVE OPENING

I had a friend who was a local beekeeper to help me this time. She had a great deal more experience than I had. I needed to know if my bees were doing okay.

Two important things ;-
1. they've almost finished the sugar syrup – in three days!
2. they now have <u>five</u> frames of brood!

Frame 4 heavy with stores
Frames 5-9 brood (9 has <u>tiny</u> eggs!)
Frame 10 is now stores
Frame 11 now completely drawn out on one side.

My diagram for the day looked like this :-

12	11	10	9	8	7	6	5	4	3	2	1
								s			
	d		t					t	d		
	r	s	i					o	r		
	a	t	n	b	b	b	b	r	a		
	w	o	y	o	r	r	r	e	w		
x	n	r		o	o	o	o	s	n	x	x
		e	e	r	o	o	o	!	o		
	o	s	g	d	d	d	d	l	o		
	u		g					o	u		
	t		s					t	t		
								s			
								!			

There are definitely <u>more</u> bees now. They seemed agitated with my friend there and I was moving a bit faster too as it was cloudy and not that warm. Overall they were good. my friend declared them healthy and happy.

I am stunned and excited by the changes I see. In <u>three</u> days!

Because of the numbers of varroa mites I had been counting and in order to give my bees a proper chance of surviving their first winter, I went against everything I believed in and inserted Bayvarol strips into the hive.

When I checked on my bees early the next morning, there were <u>dozens</u> of bees underneath the hive. Had they been there all night? Lots of bees were outside and underneath, noisy and agitated.

I needed advice.

After a long discussion with a local beekeeper, he agreed that the Bayvarol may be aggravating the bees. The only way I would know would be to remove the strips.

On the afternoon of the 19th, having anxiously watched my bees becoming more and more agitated, I opened the hive again and removed the strips. By evening there were fewer bees outside and overall the hive felt calmer. By the following afternoon they were completely back to normal.

Now, if I leap gleefully into the realm of pure whimsy (which I admit I do most happily), I might be tempted to say that my bees were agitated because I was agitated. When I got them I had promised them that I would treat them naturally and holistically and in accordance with biodynamic principles. In my own mind, using Bayvarol strips was a complete betrayal of that promise, and it was easy to believe that my own complex emotions were adversely affecting my bees.

What I know for a fact, though, is that they reacted strongly to the chemicals in the hive. Basically, when the strips went in, the bees moved out. When the strips were removed, the bees all went home again.

20.9.09

Lots of activity today because it's sunny and warm. Foragers are bringing in loads of pollen, orange and lemon yellow.

I must check the syrup in two days.

I have given the bees access to the roof space around the syrup container. It's too hard to move them away from the bucket so I left them.

21.9.09

Another inaugural flight today, lots of orienteering.

22.9.09

Bees busy and normal. Lovely to watch them coming home in the evening. Less pollen today.

A posse of bees has taken up a position underneath the hive – my research tells me that this may be to help regulate the temperature under the brood.

23.9.09

I realised last night (yet another sleepless night thinking about my bees) that the cluster of bees was <u>directly</u> underneath the hole in the crown board which I had left open the last time I checked the syrup! How thick am I?!

I replaced the piece of wood today. Let's see if the bees under the hive remove themselves.

When I checked later, they had, but only temporarily. Hmmm.

Hive Opening –

It was great to see that in one week the bees have drawn out and filled frame 12, and filled frame 11. Boy, they're working <u>hard</u>!

I suddenly realised this evening that I must give them another frame while this good weather holds. Frame 1 to position 12 tomorrow!

Very few bees underneath the hive today.

24.9.09

Right. Today I did the frame exchange so Frame 1 is now in position 12. (What this means is that the frame which was furthest back - and closest to me when I'm standing at the hive - was now at the front of the hive and in the warmest position.) I work on the premise that the more honey the bees have going into winter, the greater their chances of survival. I hope to God I'm right.

This is between me and my bees.

I fumbled the putting back of the crown board and trapped several bees. Annoyed with myself.

Overall it went well. Only a couple of bees gave me the bent eye. No following at all, even two feet away from the hive.

Now I must leave them alone for the next week.

27.9.09

I dusted from above with icing sugar again, opening gaps between the frames and letting the sugar fall on the bees. The problem with this is that the bees don't move after being dusted so it's hard to move the frames back together!

They have sacrificed frame 4 for brood; it's now stores. There's lots of honey in the brood cells. My contact was absolutely right.

I gave them a super filled with new frames of foundation wax. I will let them get on with it and see next Sunday how much progress they've made.

After I'd closed up, one bee would <u>not</u> leave me alone! She stayed with me three yards from the hive. I stood my ground. She didn't settle on me, and although I have no doubt she was looking for a way into my beesuit, she didn't find one. She really just wanted me to go away. Eventually she lost interest and buzzed home. I scarpered before she came back.

However, each time I went back to the hive after this, one single bee would appear at the sound of my voice, and fly around and around my head. Of course there was no possible way of knowing if it was the <u>same</u> bee, but it could have been! Because of her, I could no longer sit in my usual chair in peace; I would stand motionless behind the hive with my eyes closed and let her get on with it. Round and round she went, barely an inch from my skin – I could sometimes feel the air from her wings, or her leg brushing against my cheek! I stood quietly, breathing and thinking calm thoughts, until this determined bee grew tired and went home.

I wasn't being harmed by the experience, but my visits to the apiary weren't nearly as much fun as they had been.

1.10.09

I have some dead bees this morning. The feeling from the hive is lethargic, confused. I'm trying not too panic. Time for research.

3.10.09

Today everything appears completely normal. I must put the past two days into perspective so I can learn from them. On Wednesday my bees were fine. On Thursday morning there were dead bees all over the ground around the hive. Well, I thought they were dead. They were not! I had gathered them up in a pot, but several of them started moving around. I took them back to the hive and left them there. Later I inspected, and there were still bees on the ground around the hive, most with at least one or two 'companions', other bees just standing next to them. I left them overnight, assuming they would die in the night, outside the hive.

On Friday morning, six dead bees had been taken out of the hive overnight and left on the slate landing board. The ones on the ground were mostly still alive, just unmoving. I picked one up and held her in my hand for a while, then put her on the landing board. Immediately two bees rushed into her and one picked her up, flew two feet away and pushed her into the grass. I began to wonder if these strangely quiet bees hadn't been a robbing party who'd been overwhelmed and subdued. The behaviour was so strange, I couldn't get a handle on what might be going on.

Thankfully there were still many bees bringing pollen back to the hive – apparently this is a good sign.

Today, there are no more dead bees, and the hive acts as though the past two days never happened. It is all very strange. One good thing to come out of this, though, is that the one bee determined to plague me has vanished. I can again sit by my hive unmolested. A pleasure.

4.10.09

Hive Opening – last of the year

I dusted with icing sugar, top-down, between the frames. The bees were really good this time and hardly got in the way at all. Fantastic evidence of hard work, eggs plus stores. <u>Plus</u> they have drawn out six frames of the foundation in the super! Masses of bees in the super, all busy. No stores there yet, but I'm sure it won't be long.

Overall, I worked fairly fast because it wasn't as warm as I would have liked, and the bees were great. No following at all this time.

Good feeling, calm, industrious.

16.10.09

Wow! There are so many bees around the hive this afternoon, I might think they were about to swarm!

Another orientation flight? I wonder. They didn't seem agitated – I could get fairly close – they were just very noisily doing whatever they were doing.

16.10.09

At 6 p.m. I took this photograph of the underneath of my hive --

Why???

I showed this photograph to every beekeeper I could find, but no one could give me a definitive answer. Everyone who looked at it asked the same question I had: Why? It was considered extraordinary behaviour, particularly given that there are obviously foraging bees underneath the hive with pollen sacks still full from their day's work. Under normal circumstances, they should have returned to the hive and off-loaded their gatherings, both pollen and nectar. My own research suggested lack of ventilation in the hive, although I felt the bees gathering in such great numbers would create more HEAT, and I wasn't entirely comfortable with that theory.

17.10.09

This morning when I visited the hive, one bee shot out from under the hive and landed on my left forearm, stinging me immediately. Ouch! I slapped her and threw her far away, then used a fingernail to rub out the sting. I was slightly shocked that a bee had come at me with the sole intention of stinging me.

I suited up around 3 p.m. Carefully lifting the lid, I looked to see what was going on inside. In the super, 8 frames are now fully drawn out with stores in at least three of them, if not more. No activity in frames 1 – 3, but they're already busy in frame 12. Maybe later in the week I should move frame 1 to position 12 to give them more to work with?

Lots of bees. Lots and lots. Almost impossible to put the crown board back! I tried this way and that, but it was very hard not to trap them.

There are still hundreds – if not thousands – of bees underneath the hive. I wish I knew what is going on.

22.10.09

Last night I had swept the patio around the hive so it was clear of dead and dying bees. This morning it was still clear, so no bees had perished outside overnight. However, after a day of heavy showers and intermittent sunshine, when I went to check on them around 5 p.m. there were many bees on the ground, all waterlogged and still.

I picked one up and was horrified to see a huge varroa mite on her back! Tomorrow I will gather up the dead bees and see how many have varroa on them.

Awful. I feel really upset.

On the plus side, though, the bees are very active and plenty of pollen is coming in to the hive, so there are babies to be fed.

Big note though: Yesterday when I was watching, a bee dragged out a dead pupa. Horrid to see. I had to convince myself it was just the one. I saw no others today.

26.10.09

I gathered up half a dozen wet bees and brought them indoors to dry out. I gave them some honey. (Yes, I **know** you're not supposed to, but I did.) They all ate with varying degrees of enthusiasm. One in particular was strong and active, more so after some honey. Two others also perked up. When they were all moving around and the strongest one was flying under the glass, I took them all outside. The two very active ones sat on the landing slate outside the entrance to the hive. One immediately went inside. Within seconds, the one on the landing strip was jumped on, grabbed and thrown into the long grass. Almost immediately after this, another bee was airlifted out of the hive and also dumped in the grass. Both bees stayed where they'd been put.

Now. I have a theory about this. I think old bees are banished / expelled from the hive and left to die. I can see no other reason why apparently healthy bees, both able to fly, would be ejected and forcibly pushed down into the grass and left there.

15.11.09

Looking up into the hive from underneath, I could see many dead bees on the mesh floor. Dead bees were being brought out of the hive, but only a few at a time. There seemed to be dozens that needed to be removed.

I suited up, took out the one drawing pin holding the mesh closed at the rear of the hive, and pulled the mesh down with one finger. Using a bracken stalk, I flicked out as many dead bees as I could.

Oh oh oh! There were so many of them! A hundred? More? I didn't dare to count! I dumped them away from the hive. Almost immediately four dead (or dying) bees were brought out the front entrance. Inspired by my efforts? A more manageable problem? Who knows.

I used the yellow mite board to block up the gap between the blocks under the hive. I felt sure the wind must whistle up underneath the hive. I hope they will be more comfortable.

I will check the floor of the hive in one week. If there are significant numbers of dead bees, I think I have no choice but to send a sample off for testing.

If they <u>are</u> diseased, I must assume they came with it. I have had these bees for only three months, and there are no other bees nearby. Where could they have got disease from?

17.11.09

I don't want to write these notes, but I must.

Yesterday, while I was watching, the bees removed two bees from the hive; one was alive but with obviously stunted and deformed wings; the other a white pupa, almost fully grown.

Whimsical I may be, but I cannot believe the bees produced these two obviously defective bees just for my benefit. I must assume they are just two in a long line of evictions on that day.

I believe now that my bees are not well, that they are over-run by disease, and that they will not survive the winter.

I cannot help them – they have clustered now (mostly; they still seem to be foraging a bit) and any treatment will not reach the centre of the colony, most especially the queen.

This weekend I will gather a sample and send them for testing with a letter expressing my thoughts.

20.11.09

Change of plan. I have decided to reintroduce the Bayvarol strips. I know they will have lost some of their effectiveness because the packet has been open for weeks. However, even if they work at 25%, that gives my bees 25% more chance of making it through the winter.

> This was a very difficult decision for me and went against everything I believed in. However, I was deeply distressed by what I was seeing and was utterly convinced my bees wouldn't survive the winter without my help. I could see no alternative. I was scared. Today, I know my bees better and believe in them more. I would not do this again.

Today I opened the hive again – the first good weather we've had in weeks – and I worked fast because it was cold (only 10°C). Lots of bees. Very encouraging. Lots and lots of bees! The super was so heavy I could barely lift it! Masses of honey.

I got the strips in and closed up, really heartened by the number of bees. When I checked under the hive, there were <u>no more dead bees</u>! This is really great news. I am so relieved. I feel much more optimistic now.

I must remove the Bayvarol strips by Friday, 1st January. So between Christmas and New year, the first fine day .....

At the entrance, there is normal activity, lots of coming and going, and the bees are <u>still</u> bringing pollen in, two different colours. Very exciting.

29.11.09

Well, the weather changed quite suddenly, the temperature dropping sharply. After a week of torrential rain, suddenly there was snow on the mountains and we're all in polonecks! It's barely been over 3° or 4° C during the day.

Of course my bees have clustered seriously now; they have virtually disappeared. And of course I was caught on the hop!

I put an old cushion cover, stuffed with a square of dense foam from an old exercise mat, on top of the crown board for insulation, and covered the entire hive with an old tumble-drier cover which is open at the front. This will protect the hive on three sides and should keep out the worst of the west, south-west and north-west winds. Unfortunately it won't protect the hive from the east wind but the entrance to the hive is small and the bees should be safe.

When the weather is drier (heavy rain today) I will tie sections of exercise mat around the hive (inside the tumble-drier cover) to insulate it from the worst winds.

I don't know what more I can do.

2.12.09

It's a lovely day today with still air and sunshine! Only about 7° - 8°C but that didn't stop my bees. They were out in force, enjoying the fresh air! It is wonderful to see them looking so vigorous and perky.

I used yoga mats to insulate the hive today, and put the drier cover over the top. As much as I need do, I think.

Today I blocked the entrance to the hive using a tuft of grass. The bees were indoors (4 p.m.) except for one guard bee who kept popping out to see what I was up to. The grass was effective and <u>very</u> easy to use. I needed to do it for myself and now I won't forget.

Once the entrance was blocked up, I could move around the hive in complete comfort.

4.12.09

I checked on my bees today, lifting off the covering and looking up into the hive from underneath the mesh floor.

I was <u>very</u> happy to see that -

a) the floor of the hive is clean as a whistle; and
b) there are <u>lots</u> of bees, all active, vigorous and noisy.

I spoke to them and a 'whoosh' went through the colony as they all perked up and started moving around.

If they are moving back and forth in the brood chamber, all the more chance the Bayvarol will get to all the bees, and the greater the chance that it will actually work!

11.12.09

My bees were out and about yesterday – sunny and still, 10

Out today too, cloudy, breezy, and only 8°. Good to see them again.

28.12.09

I removed the Bayvarol strips today. Too cold, I know, but the week is due to get much colder. It couldn't wait.

I worked as fast as I could. Lots of bees! It was reassuring to see so many at this time of year.

However, any bee which flew out of the hive almost immediately fell to the ground. It was cold, and although I was working quickly the exercise cost me many bees. They lay all around me on the patio - maybe as many as a hundred dead bees. A high price.

1.1.10

I went to wish my bees a Happy New Year. They haven't been doing any housework this week, so I wanted to check on them.

There are still enough bees to make a fair noise when I started talking to them.

2.1.10

Today I gave my bees some fondant. I put it in a small Tupperware box so I'll be able to see what they're up to through the plastic. It's not much (about 500gms) but I'm interested to see what they do with it. I'll check in a week.

They certainly made a big sound when I spoke to them, and there was lots of activity.

I did a 24-hour 'natural fall' mite check using the yellow plastic boards underneath the hive. I almost couldn't believe my eyes: <u>Zero</u> mites. Not a one!

13.1.10

The temperature rose slightly today and in the afternoon the sun shone! I got home at around 3.15 fully prepared to chase my bees out for a cleansing flight – to find them all out and about already! Clever girls!

Lots of bees, all looking well. I sat in my usual chair and only one bee came up to see who I was, flew around my head a couple of times, and then went back to the hive. Otherwise they ignored me completely.

20.1.10

With the weather a few degrees warmer, my bees have been flying virtually every afternoon. It's been fantastic to see them out and about.

But yesterday they were bringing in dark orange <u>pollen</u>! I couldn't believe it. Does this mean the queen is laying already?

24.1.10

I finally got round to lifting the lid and checking on the fondant. The Tupperware container was utterly clean, as if it had been through the wash. All the fondant had been consumed. I gave the bees what I had left and promised to buy them some more.

27.1.10

The bees are out and about every day now, even today with the temperature hovering around 6°. I sat looking at the hive for a short while in the early morning, and a scout returned so I'm sure they'll be flying later.

Tonight is the first bee federation meeting of the new year. I must ask –

Would the queen be laying this early? And
What can I do with any honey left over after the winter?

At the bee meeting I spoke at length to other beekeepers who patiently answered my questions. In the first instance, the queen could be laying although at this stage the amount of brood would be small, in February things really take off; and in the second instance, left-over honey is more likely to be ivy honey and might have crystalised. If not, however, yes, I could harvest it.

I asked one beekeeper with four decades of experience behind him where drones come from, drones to mate with your own young virgin queen. He told me about 'drone corridors' in the sky. These have existed for millennia, he told me, what he called 'pathways in the sky' that the bees have used for hundreds and hundreds of years, the drones searching for a queen to mate with. If I have a young queen ready for mating, he said, the drones will appear.

Given that the summer before I got my bees we had a couple of honeybees on flowers in the garden, there could very well be a feral swarm / nest nearby which would be perfect – if they survived this winter (a particularly long and cold one) they'll be naturally more resilient. It would be interesting to see if they were 'wilder' though ….!

> I was making a lot of mistakes and I'm sure I was doing things which would make an experienced beekeeper roll their eyes in exasperation, but at the bee meeting I had learned that many very experienced beekeepers had lost between 30% - 50% of their hives that winter. My bees had survived. Whatever I was doing wrong, I was also doing something right.

8.2.10

Today was cold (no higher than 2°C all day – brrrr!) but over the past couple of weeks as soon as the temperature's gone up – with sun – the bees have been out. Their minimum flying temperature seems to be between 6 - 8°C.

10.2.10

There are bees bringing pollen in and it's only 6° !

14.2.10

More pollen coming in, 6 - 6½°C.

15.2.10

One forager came home as I was watching, pollen sacks full with orange pollen. Only just 6° again.

I'm painting hive 2. I'm happier with this one.

26.2.10

There was lots of activity yesterday. It looked like more orientation flights. At least it was warm and still. Today the wind is howling and it's barely above 6°, but still my girls were out and returning with great loads of pollen. I'm amazed they can fly into this wind! I saw one bee emerge, wipe her antennae, feel the day and then go back inside! Shortly after that four of them emerged together and took off.

Yesterday I watched a bee in a different part of the garden. She was flying over the grass and settling, walking deep between the blades of grass and back out again. I wondered if she was collecting water from the grass. I couldn't think what else she could be doing.

I have since watched this behaviour many times and have learned that collecting water from the grass is exactly what that bee was doing. This happens particularly after a light drizzle. My bees have access to water in many different places, but they definitely prefer to collect their own in this way.

14.3.10

I have to write these notes <u>immediately</u> – while I'm still euphoric!!

Today I deemed it warm enough to open the hive. I carefully lifted the lid, removed the insulating cushion and gently removed the two blocks of wood covering the holes in the crown board. There were bees on the inside of the middle block so I rested this on the landing board and these bees quickly made their way inside. Softly, softly, I lifted the crown board. No propolis. No panic. The bees were quiet and settled.

I lifted out the first frame (undrawn) and worked forward from there. Frame 3 was drawn but empty. From frames 4 forwards, all frames were filled and sealed, stores. <u>Beautiful</u>! I went no further. Because the bees were barely moving I could return the crown board easily. Blocks back on over the holes, lid on, all complete.

Excellent !!!

I put the mite board back under the hive for another free-fall mite count. 24-hours turned into 48+ because I forgot – but ZERO mites <u>again</u> !!!

21.3.10

It's the warmest day of the year so far! 12°! Still chilly with a strong wind, so I didn't open the hive.

The bees were incredibly active and <u>masses</u> of dark orange pollen is coming in. They've found a good source somewhere.

It's wonderful to hear the activity, even from two yards away. I often hear bees around the garden now. Lots of scouting.

24.3.10

I went into the super during the afternoon and moved the two rearmost frames – undrawn – into the centre to see if they will start working on them. If they do, I should be able to remove the honey-filled frames one by one, replacing them with foundation wax for them to draw. I hope to be able to harvest some of last year's honey this way. I don't know if I can – or <u>should</u> – try this.

I realised afterwards that I had probably done <u>completely the wrong thing</u> by changing the order of the frames because they are all drawn out to differing depths. By removing frames I could be reducing the bee-space between them, possibly even trapping bees. I needed to go back in and take one (honey) frame out completely to compensate for this.

26.3.10

I went in today (two days later) and reversed what I had done.

Having done some research, I have learned that I cannot remove honey-filled frames one by one, so I must give the bees another super. What I need to know now is whether I can put the new super under the honey-filled one or whether it <u>must</u> go <u>above</u>.

It is worth recording that the two frames of undrawn foundation wax were covered with bees. They want to work – I must give them room to do so.

27.3.10

I went in again (how forgiving my bees are!) only to add a super and the five frames I had just built. As soon as I removed the central block covering the hole in the crown board, they were through. They <u>definitely</u> needed more space!

I have left the crown board where it was with the central hole open. I will remove it completely when I've assembled the rest of the frames. Soon, soon.

3.4.10

I opened up today to add four more newly assembled frames - BUT not one single bee was in the super on the new frames. Not one.

So. Either they don't need the space and aren't interested <u>or</u> the crown board is stopping them from moving up.

What do I think I should do?

I'm going to leave it until a proper fine day, and then I can examine the whole hive and make a decision.

Or should I just remove the crown board and see what happens?

Time. Sleep. Think.

4.4.10

I removed the crown board today. Let's see what they do now. I must leave them entirely alone for a week.

6.4.10

I got stung today! Hotziggedy I was annoyed! A bee heard my voice from inside the hive, shot out the front entrance, zoomed at my face like a bullet and stung me on the forehead, just above the eyebrow. Full intent. No hesitation.

Note to self: These are not pets. They are not 'tame'. And they do a <u>very</u> good job of reminding!

> Is anyone surprised I got stung? Of course not! I had invaded my bees' space repeatedly over the previous few weeks, and as I spoke to my bees continuously when I worked with them, it should have come as no surprise to me that they might recognise and react adversely to the sound of my voice!

10.4.10

Hive opening today. Only one frame of the new super is drawn out. This is a surprise.

In the old super <u>most of the honey has been removed</u> from the frames! It's almost completely empty. There is a small amount of <u>brood</u> in one frame. What <u>is</u> she up to?

In the brood chamber I was very surprised to find only <u>two and a half frames</u> of brood. There are some eggs, so the queen is still around somewhere. I didn't spend time looking for her.

So little brood? I can only hope that I have peeked in at a transitional moment, that all those empty cells are about to be filled.

All brood is workers. No potential queen cells. No drones.

Lots of bees, all trying to kill me for interfering! But as soon as I closed up they were quiet and disappeared. No following at all.

I had to use the water spray to get the super back on.

Mostly the bees were feisty in the supers, gentle in the brood chamber.

Overall successful, but I am confused and perplexed by the lack of brood. I hope next week will present a different picture.

What surprised me most was that the honey was <u>gone</u>. In less than a month that super has gone from full to almost empty. Why?

I was particularly intrigued by frame 1 of the super. It is not drawn out at all but glistened with moisture, top to bottom. I dabbed my finger in it and tasted. Water. An in-house water store! I haven't heard of or read about anything like this. Fascinating.

How on earth do the bees store water on a <u>vertical</u> surface?

17.4.10

Hive opening today. The weather was gorgeous so I didn't have to rush at all.

All was calm and smooth. I was pleased to see a great improvement in the amount of brood – queenie's gone from 2½ frames of brood to 7 frames in one week! And finally, DRONE BROOD!!

The first super is now fully utilised for brood, so I have taken to calling it the 'brood super'. I put the queen excluder between the brood super and the honey super. I checked carefully to see if the queen was up there (only a few bees, so not too hard) but must go in again in a couple of days to make sure there's no sign of her above the excluder.

Overall my bees were co-operative and well-behaved. They were easy to move with a few squirts of water spray, and only one bee flew directly at my face and pinged off my veil.

A bumble bee caused a moment's problem, but I swatted it away. More worrying was the <u>wasp</u> which got into the super, between the frames. I hope I flicked it out, but I'm not entirely sure …

I meant to include a 24-hour mite check three days ago. Still NIL. None. Nothing but pollen mites and general hive debris. Can there <u>really</u> be no mites at all?

19.4.10

I'm euphoric again! It's cloudy and cooler today, but I felt I <u>had</u> to check the super to make absolutely sure I hadn't trapped the queen.

Lots of bees in the super, busy-busy-busy. A beautiful perfect honey store – already with honey in it, since Saturday! All in all, in perfect pristine condition. Almost as if, without the queen's presence, the workers have excelled themselves. No sign of her anywhere, thank heavens. All good.

I lifted out several frames to have a careful look (for eggs) and the bees were completely still. Several were head-down, tail-up, deep within the cells. But they were <u>so</u> well-behaved. They barely even noticed me!

No problem returning the crown board – except that many of them came up through the slot as soon as it was in place. I sprayed them with a little water, and when they'd gone back down I slid the block in place.

Excellent !!

29.4.10

Today, finally, it was calm enough and warm enough to do the hive swap I've been mentally planning for weeks. I wanted to transfer all the frames from the older white hive into the freshly painted blue hive, so I could repaint the white hive.

But horror of horrors! What do I find? The queen WAS trapped on the wrong side of the queen excluder and had started laying in the tiny honey cells! Oh NO! What a monumental mistake.

In the brood chamber below the bees had tried to make a new queen (finding themselves queenless) but had been unsuccessful. All the lower cells were empty with only a little unhatched worker brood.

I had to rejig everything. The honey super now became the brood super, and vice versa. I hope to goodness my queen is still below the queen excluder. I need to check this weekend to make sure she's laying in the brood chambers, otherwise I don't know what I'll do.

Dear Lord, what a stuff up!

I realised later that the only way to deal with this is to remove the excluder and give the queen the run of the hive. This I have done. Long term? I don't know, but for now I feel better about it.

4.5.10

Hive opening today. Only just warm enough I felt, but some sun.

I lifted off the top super with the crown board *in situ* and placed it on the lid. Then I covered the middle super with a pillow case (to keep the bees warm and calm) and put that on top of the first super. Then I went through the brood chamber. Mostly stores now.

I replaced the middle super and went through it. Some brood, some honey. Not a huge amount of either. But, great excitement, on frame 8 - **I SAW THE QUEEN !!!** Wow, she is beautiful, dark and sleek and shiny, and twice the length of the workers. Quite magnificent.

When I replaced the top super and went through it, I found it has reverted almost completely to a honey store and so *because I knew where the queen was* (and I double-checked!) I reintroduced the queen excluder.

I also saw a drone, a great brute of a fellow, getting in the way. AND I saw a bee doing the waggle dance!

All in all it went very well. Quite a few bees tried to make me go away and one stung my glove (but thankfully not me) and they were feistier in the brood chamber than the middle super where the queen was. But overall they were well-behaved. Nothing a little spray of water couldn't cure.

I'm a little surprised the queen isn't laying more. I hope that if I can leave them alone for a week to 10 days, she will get back into the swing of things.

9.5.10

Hive opening today – 3 o'clock or thereabouts – and what should I find in the top super? Four frames of brood! Sealed and unsealed.

Madam queen can definitely get through the excluder!

Oh boy. The hive is now a complete mess, set up as follows :

Top super: four frames of brood
Middle super: five frames of brood
Brood chamber: two frames of brood

There are two frames heavy with stores in the brood chamber, and frame 6, 10 and 11 have lots of pollen stores.

Overall the workers were very good. The <u>drones</u> tried to rally the troops, but apart from a couple of persistent guards, they were calm and still on the comb. I couldn't find the queen this time – and I really tried to find her! – but I saw some small larvae so I know she's in there somewhere.

I felt much more competent this time, even though I'm not always 100% sure what I'm looking at. I don't think I inadvertently killed any bees this time either, which pleases me.

I inserted the yellow board for a 24-hour mite count. Will check tomorrow.

10.5.10

Zero mites. Again. This is the fifth time.

15.5.10

Another hive opening.

Now a fully operational hive of three levels.

<u>In the top super</u>: 4 frames of brood, all sealed, including in the fifth frame a queen cell, right in the middle! Not sealed yet. Lots of stores, and they're drawing out frames 3 and 11. All fine and good.

<u>In the middle super</u>: 5 frames of brood, 2 of eggs (one tiny!).

<u>In the brood chamber</u>: 3 frames of brood. Pollen stores.

Overall the worker bees were excellent, the drones were a pain, one determined to incite a riot but completely ignored. Generally they were still and quiet, utterly unconcerned by my presence. At one stage it was almost as if I wasn't really there. It was silent and calm. Then that bloody drone tried to stir things up again…

I **saw the queen** again. Very happy.

In total, 12 frames of brood. And the queen cell. Hmmm….. What do I do about it?

<u>Options</u>:
Destroy it
Artificial swarm
Move queen cell into another hive
Give it away (?)
Let them swarm and hope to catch.

16.5.10

Today my beekeeping friend came round and we went through the hive together. There were <u>lots</u> of potential queen cells – at least 3 in the top super, 4 in the middle chamber – <u>in addition</u> to the well-formed almost sealed cell in top super, frame 5.

Choices to make.

As I am not equipped to deal with queen rearing (nor even remotely experienced enough, in my opinion), the other potential queen cells had to be torn down. Destroyed.

This was hard.
And I hated every second of it.

The top super is now **Hive No 2,** with its own floor, crown board and roof. All the bees in the top super must now form their own colony and rear their new queen.

If they don't all fly 'home' when I open the entrance in three days time, there is a chance it will work. Finding themselves queenless, they will put all their efforts into rearing a new queen. If she mates successfully in a few weeks' time, all systems go for Hive No 2.

For now, they are closed in. They have ventilation through the mesh floor and I will feed them sugar syrup tonight (1-1) and give them wet leaves in case they need water.

And I will pray.

For the colony in Hive No 1, I must check in a few days that there are new eggs and that my precious queen is still in that hive. We couldn't find her today. More prayers!

17.5.10

I just opened Hive No 1 to add the brand new super I'd assembled this morning. I also had a look for the queen in the middle super but couldn't see her anywhere. I didn't intrude further (to look in the lower reaches) – I'll have a proper look towards the end of the week.

Added the super and closed up.

Now I have to say that my bees were so good the whole event seems never to have happened. I didn't have to use the water spray once. They barely moved! Extraordinary considering we made an extensive incursion into their sacred lands yesterday.

I don't think I'll sleep properly until I see the queen. It's worrying me. In addition, I find I am emotionally unprepared to have a second hive. I feel a bit odd about it. I think that after I've positioned it properly, it may feel better.

19.5.10

I opened Hive 1 today, still looking for Her Elusive Majesty. Still no sign of her. No new eggs, small lavae – could they have been laid before we split the hive? No tiny eggs to be seen.

Late afternoon my son alerted me to bees coming out of Hive 2. I suited up and went to see. Sure enough, the entrance block had moved (been moved? by the bees?) enough for them to squeeze through. I turned the block to give them back their doorway and noticed distinct signs of gnawing on the wood!

Bees are coming out of Hive 2, but they're orienting themselves and going back in. Phew! 5 p.m. seems a pretty good time, too, as they'll be settling down for the night fairly soon.

Tomorrow I <u>have</u> to go into Hive 2 to see if the queen is there.

Later, no activity around Hive 2. None at all. Hive 1 is busy as usual, later afternoon on a warm sunny day.

Now I'm worried that all the bees from Hive 2 have gone home to Hive 1.

9 p.m. I went out to check. I knocked sharply on the front of Hive 2 and was rewarded with a significant 'fizz' from inside. I looked up into the hive from underneath and could see lots of bees.

Perhaps we're going to be okay.

20.5.10

Well, it all started innocently enough ….

I opened Hive 2 specifically to look for the queen who I <u>knew</u> was hiding in there somewhere. Backwards and forwards I went through the frames – Aha! There she was! I tried to catch her and she took off at a run, and promptly vanished. Bugger!

Backwards and forwards I went through the frames lifting out each one and examining it in minute detail. Backwards and forwards. Again! Backwards and forwards! I stopped seeing bees. I saw the queen everywhere, and nowhere. Eventually I gave up and prepared to close the hive.

I lifted the crown board to close up and there, with only two attendants, my precious queen! All exposed and in the open!

I immediately put the crown board back on the ground where I had found it (gently, gently…!) and opened Hive 1. With the chambers exposed, I lifted the crown board and held it over the hive. I gently nudged her majesty off. She immediately disappeared down between the frames.

Hive 1 has its queen!

Hive 2 has potential queen cells.

All closed up. And me all a-quiver!

I don't know if this is going to work, but at least my queen is where she belongs.

Phew!

23.5.10

Oh boy, I am utterly exhausted! But where to start?

I opened Hive 2 and scanned the brood nest. I couldn't see anything that looked like a viable queen cell. They've tried to build but with no eggs to fill.

I closed up and opened Hive 1. There were two frames with several queen cells. Knowing that my queen was still in Hive 1, I shook the bees off these two frames completely and transferred them to Hive 2.

I closed up, thinking now Hive 1 has its queen; Hive 2 has strong potential.

Satisfied.

Not half an hour later my husband called me.

They had swarmed !!!

Back into my beesuit (such a hot day!), armed with a cardboard box, my secateurs and wearing my proper bee gauntlets, I tackled the hedgerow where they were resting.

The roar of a swarm is the most extraordinary, exciting and <u>intimidating</u> sound. It is nothing like the gentle hum of a working hive, nor the frenetic buzzing of angry bees. These are bees that mean serious business.

Whether the queen makes the decision to leave and leads the way, or whether the workers take that decision upon themselves and push the queen to swarm, I know not. It is an extraordinary sight and getting close to the swarm and dealing with it took courage I didn't know I had.

Somehow I got most of them into the box, closed it up and put it under the pear tree in the shade.

As Hive 2 was virtually empty of bees (the colony was really very small) and as the bees were all sisters, I had no hesitation in dumping the swarm into Hive 2. I added a chamber on top and closed up.

Mix-and-match bees. I don't even know if I <u>can</u> or <u>should</u> do what I did. But it's done.

When I spoke to my friend later, she said I must destroy the queen cells in Hive 1 – all but one of them – if I can't find the queen. Otherwise they'll just swarm again.

Back into my beesuit. I opened Hive 1.

This time I shook bees off the frames (after checking for a queen) so I could see properly. Oh my God! There were queen cells everywhere! I tore them off – hated it – and left only one. I didn't see a queen.

In total I must have destroyed ten potential queens. This is wrong wrong wrong.

I must be better prepared and in a position to pass on these potential queens to other people. I'm supposed to be preserving the honeybee, not killing it.

I'm ordering nuc boxes so I can remove frames with queen cells and give them away.

24.5.10

I wonder if they'll swarm again today ….

"A swarm in May is worth a load of hay …"

(traditional verse)

25.5.10

The bees in Hive 2 have pushed / pulled <u>in</u> the entrance block. Why would they do this?

26.5.10

I definitely saw one bee enter Hive 2 with pollen. Another later in the day. Dare I think they're settling?

29.5.10

I went to check on them. The weather was damp and drizzly (at last!). All very quiet in Hive 2, no sign of anyone. I knocked, but no guard bee appeared. I looked up from underneath but couldn't see any bees. So I knocked again, and this time there was a strong 'fizzzzz..' from inside. So there <u>are</u> bees in there. Phew!

30.5.10

Hive opening.

Hive 1:
Brood chamber – some brood still to hatch, otherwise stores.
Brood super – some brood still to hatch excellent stores, +++ frame 6 at least 3 or 4 sealed queen cells on each side! Lots of attention being paid to these.

But obviously no queen.

Hive 2:
Bees tense, agitated.
Possible queen cell on frame 8, otherwise no evidence of a queen.

No work at all in the brood chamber which is sitting on top of the super.

So. They HAD swarmed again. Two queenless hives. I am really sad to have lost my beautiful queen. Now I wait and see what happens.

1.6.10

For the first time today there was what I would consider normal activity from Hive 2. Lots of coming and going, lots of pollen going in – including green pollen from bluebells. Also a couple of 'Diwali' bees – bees which have gathered nectar from a flower which has showered them with pollen, leaving them looking like an explosion of light.

The whole feeling from the hive was much more optimistic.

I spoke at length to my wonderfully useful beekeeper friend. She's coming round tomorrow and we'll open the hives and see what's really going on. She did say that it seemed likely a queen <u>had</u> hatched in Hive 2, and that she'd be hard to spot pre-mating because she'd be much the same size as the workers.

Hive 1 is busy busy busy.

2.6.10

Hive 2: The bees were calm, noticeably so. At least one, possibly two hatched queens. We were happy to leave them be. I closed up.

Hive 1: The marked frame (frame 6) was covered in queen cells! We put that aside for my friend to take away with her in a nuc box. I also cut out three clustered queen cells from frame 5 and, using a tooth-pick, attached these to frame 6.

We looked at the queen cell I had seen on frame 7 – now open! – and on frame 8 **there she was!!** <u>So</u> exciting to see her. My young queen, so perfect, agile, restless, beautiful. I closed up, really happy.

Two queenright hives. Brilliant!

I noted that in Hive 1 there were <u>many</u> more bees than there had been on Sunday. The brood chamber was <u>full</u> of bees! I had heard that if a swarm loses its queen, the bees may come home again. It looks as though this is exactly what has happened.

N.B. I must make 6 more frames to fill the super in Hive 1.

What a fantastic day !

7.6.10

I added a super to Hive 1 today as there are so many bees in there they will definitely need more space. (It was pouring with rain and I wasn't sure how I was going to do this until my husband suggested using the sun umbrella. What a champion! He even held it steady for me!)

8.6.10

I was keen to open Hive 2 to see how many bees were in there – and it was a great relief to see lots of bees. I looked for a queen but couldn't see her. This was a disappointment because I still don't know for sure that there _is_ one.

I opened Hive 1. There were a few bees resting in super 3, but no work yet of course. Good stores in super 2 already.

I put the queen excluder between supers 1 and 2 (having first checked on the position of my queen – I'm not making **that** mistake again! – and I saw her again, on frame 8. Such a thrill!).

13.6.10

I opened Hive 2 first. I couldn't find a queen. No evidence of laying. There seemed to be lots of drones in the hive. I don't know where they all came from. Still no activity at all in the brood chamber.

> I spent a lot of time thinking about these additional drones. If, when a virgin queen takes her mating flight, only the drones that actually mate with her die, perhaps drones follow her back to her hive and just move in. This would explain their sudden appearance.

In Hive 1, I couldn't spot the queen today, and there was still no evidence of laying. Lots of bees, getting feistier the lower I went. Positively angry in the brood chamber! One bee stayed with me all the time, around my face, trying to drive me away. I finally managed to spray water at her and she flew off. Lots of bees, but I was disturbed not to find the queen today. I hope she's okay.

20.6.10

Hive opening :-

Hive 2 –
Laying? No
Queen? No
Numbers? Hmmmm
Stores + pollen
No more brood to hatch.

Hive 1 –

Laying? No

Queen? No

Numbers? Lots. As many as before? I don't know, maybe not. Frames 7 and 8 have cells which shine. Could this be in preparation for laying?

No more brood to hatch.

Overall it went very well. No bees pinged against my veil; no one tried to kill me, or even made me go away. All calm in the sun.

It worries me that I can't find the queen/s. Did she go on her mating flight and get lost? Taken by a bird?

We go away tomorrow for ten days. All will have to wait until we return. Hopefully there will be a different picture.

1.7.10

Back from England. Late. I went to visit my girls. Gave Hive 2 a strident knock and was happy to hear a significant roar from inside. Dare I hope?

2.7.10

Hive opening today. Did Hive 2 first. O.M.G!!!!

!!! Brood everywhere !!!

Frames 4 – 11 brood – huge laying! – so eight – yes EIGHT! – frames of brood! Most sealed, some larvae, some eggs.

Excellent!! Happy bees. Happy ME !!!

Again, all calm in the sun.

Hive 1 next:

Both supers filling up nicely – must order two more!

Brood super: frames 4 – 8 brood, rather patchy.
She's laid between the pollen and the honey stores, but <u>she's laying</u> !!!

Brood chamber: frames 6 – 10 brood. Five full frames. Frame 7 <u>fully</u> laid with sealed brood. Stunning!!!

I am on such a high! I even did a little dance! I feel like running around the garden and squealing! I can't describe how chuffed I feel.

Two Perfect Hives !!!!!

4.7.10

Today I transposed the brood chamber and the super on Hive 2. I had to do this. Queenie had laid almost end-to-end in the super, leaving the workers almost nowhere to put stores. They <u>must</u> now draw down the frames in the brood chamber to give themselves more space – for more brood, alternatively pollen and honey stores. When they've made some progress on this I'll put on another super, with queen excluder. They must build up stores if they're going to survive the winter.

They have ignored the brood chamber completely up til now. I hope this will encourage them to make use of it.

The transposing of the chambers was an easy operation with no trouble from the bees <u>at all</u>.

12.7.10

Hive opening today.

Hive 2:
Two frames now drawn in the brood chamber with honey in them already. The bees were calm, all working away.

I saw the queen today! She's very dark. Beautiful.

Hive 1:
Oh good lord! So many bees! Masses of stores in the lower chambers, could probably get away with taking both supers of honey BUT where would all those bees go? Again, bees increasingly aggressive the lower I went and positively antsy in the brood chamber.

> I realised later on that with the swarm returning to the hive, there were twice as many bees as there should have been. I ought to have lost half my bees when they swarmed, but with a young queen laying up a storm – ostensibly to replace lost bees and return the colony to its original size – suddenly the colony was much bigger than it would otherwise have been.

I couldn't see the queen in Hive 1 which was hardly surprising. Even if she'd been painted bright red I would have struggled to see her between all those bees.

I squished a few practice cells – they were no bigger than last week.

I realised afterwards that when I dismantle the hive and put the brood super on top of the honey supers I should – no MUST – put the queen excluder between them in case the queen is in the brood super and drops down.

I don't know what to do with all the bees in Hive 1. There are just so many!

> I worked out that on 30.5.10 I had two queenless hives; on 2.6.10 the queen in Hive 2 had hatched, and there was already a young queen in Hive 1 who must have hatched a day or so previously; on 20.6.10 there was no laying in the hive (so either the queens hadn't yet been mated OR more likely, they were waiting for all existing brood to hatch); and at least five days prior to my return from England, both queens had started laying. Three to three-and-a-half weeks from hatching to laying. It was a relief to me that my bees were doing at least ONE thing according to the book!

17.7.10

Okay, time to make some notes.

First off, I forgot the last time I recorded my hive opening – I can't believe I forgot!! – that **I tasted my honey !!!!** Wow! I broke some wax which the bees had built up on the top of one of the frames and then, in the sunlight, I saw a glisten on my gloved finger. I looked closely and realised what it was. Now, I'm safe in my beesuit, the hive's wide open. I'm not going to undress for anything! So I used my honey-covered fingertip to push in my veil, and sucked. Ooooooooh! It was delicious! As pale golden as sunlight and so distinctive. Quite different from the honey we buy. A fantastic experience.

Secondly, I was really surprised to see bees foraging on the climbing rose. Quickly, nipping from flower to flower, almost as if the nectar was hardly worth their while. I ran indoors for my camera, but it was really hard to catch the shot because the bees were moving so fast! It was such a lovely summer sound, though, walking under the rose-covered archway and being surrounded by the hum.

Today I did a hive opening, Hive 2 first as has become my custom.

Lots of the babies have hatched now so there are many more bees than there were the last time (I LOVE seeing the furry-faced babies!). **I saw the queen** on frame 5, quite small but perfect, her abdomen a long narrow torpedo, and very dark.

They're working very well on the brood frames, drawing out side to side to utter perfection, and building up their stores too. I think they'll go into Winter very strong.

Hive 1 is full to <u>bursting</u>! A gazillion bees! I took off the supers and had to scrape off a lot of wax build-up on the queen excluder. The bees hung on tightly to the wax as I scraped it, but I shook them off the lumps of wax and as soon as they'd gone I pocketed it.

I got the surprise of my life in the brood super when I realised that there were **two different types of bees** in there, the dark ones I'm used to, and some much yellower ones I've never seen before. Ho ho! A foreigner! An Italian! All the new bees are a different type of bee!

I wonder how often this happens? And what it means for my hive, for the colony.
My research tells me that Italian honeybees ---

are very prolific
are excellent housekeepers
use little propolis
are excellent foragers
are superb comb builders
cover their honey with <u>white</u> capping
have a lower tendency to swarm

On the downside, they ---

are more prone to robbing
consume large amounts of honey later winter / early spring
are inclined to forage closer to home
are less likely to ripen heather honey before sealing
are not suited to cool maritime regions
are not suited to areas with strong spring nectar flow (because they're slow starters).

They have a reputation for gentleness, but **if crossed with darker races can be vicious.**

Oops!

But they are so beautiful!

25.7.10

Sunday. Very warm. Humid. Hive opening today.

In Hive 2 they have filled four frames with stores and are drawing out more frames. They look set to go into Winter very strong.

In the 'brood' chamber, frames 4, 5, 7, 8, 9, 10, 11 and 12 are well packed with brood. Eight frames! Definitely more bees, lots of babies. All calm and well-behaved.

In Hive 2, I saw <u>one</u> Italian bee! She stood out like a sore thumb. She must have miscalculated on her orientation flight and wandered into the next door hive by mistake. No one was objecting to her being there, she was going about her business alongside them. I didn't see the queen today.

I was hesitant to open Hive 1, just because there were <u>so many</u> bees in there last time, and it was really hard to work around them. I took a deep breath and lifted the lid.

My Italian babies are everywhere! They are so beautiful!

There wasn't quite as much sealed honey as I had thought (I'm planning my first honey harvest) but there were definitely at least five frames in the lower super – I didn't go through the honey supers frame by frame. In the brood super, there are at least four frames with brood and stores as well. I didn't approach the brood chamber.

I squished a couple of practice swarm cells in both hives. There's no real intent, but it doesn't hurt to change their minds.

Generally it looks good all round. Only one bee hassled me a bit while I was in Hive 1, but she didn't follow me at all.

I have ordered an extractor, and as soon as it arrives I'm going to have a go at getting honey into jars. In my head I'm designing a label, something which above all else will reflect how I feel as a beekeeper.

25.7.10

My first honey harvest! I was getting so nervous about the whole procedure I knew that if I didn't just get in there and do the thing, it wouldn't happen at all. I had been told to wait for evening, but I had this instinct that I wanted the sun on the hive when I removed the honey frames and early afternoon seemed a better time to me, when the foragers would still be out and about. As I've been successfully keeping happy bees almost entirely on instinct, I was happy enough to go on gut feeling alone and that day, that moment, felt RIGHT!

I took a new super and sealed the bottom with one of the yellow mite boards, and fashioned a lid out of the other one. With this, my water bottle and my bee brush, I approached the hive. I stood for a while, trying to calm my breathing and shake off the feeling that I was about to do a BAD thing to my bees. If I did it right, all would be well. I opened up.

Looking closely at the second super, I found that although there was lots of honey in it, very little was sealed. I removed that super and put it aside. Super 1 also had several frames which were full but hadn't been sealed yet – I need to be more positive and move frames around so that the sealed frames are moved back and unsealed frames are in a more workable position. I lifted out the first fully sealed frame. It was covered with bees. I shook them but they weren't going anywhere. Gently, gently, I used the brush. They didn't like this one bit! However, once I'd started I could keep going and soon enough the frame was clean. I slid it into the lidded 'box' and closed up. Next frame.

These bees were annoyed because many of them had already been brushed off the first frame and now here was this bloody brush thing again! Several bees attacked the brush, biting at it and hanging on, trying to find something solid to sting into. I managed to shake them out of the bristles and carried on. Slowly, I kept reminding myself, slowly. Take your time. There's no rush. Be gentle.

I got five beautiful frames out of the super.

That was all, but that was enough. I sprayed the bees a bit to calm them down, and closed up. Two bees stayed with me, whizzing around my head, but they went home again fairly soon. I noticed a couple of bees on the ground nearby, youngsters who probably hadn't been outside the hive yet but who'd fallen when brushed off. I picked them up and put them on the landing board. I must remember to brush even more carefully so I don't lose babies needlessly.

I stood in the orchard for a while just breathing, and then checked inside the box, lifting out the frames and examining them carefully all over. No bees. Half way back to the house I double-checked, but there wasn't one. A definite coup. I felt quite proud of myself.

Then I phoned Mum, and got everything together. It was going to be a bit Heath Robinson but I was good at winging it with bee stuff. We would be okay. Everything was as clean as I could make it, the extractor was shiny, there were bowls, hot water on tap, and a pot of simmering water on the stove holding the knife.

My Mum arrived, and my husband hovered with my camera, I put on some gloves, and Mum held the first frame while I positioned it so that the light was perfect. Holding the heated knife, I slid it under the wax. That first cut was amazing! Instantly there was honey everywhere, running over my hands, the knife, and into the bowl.

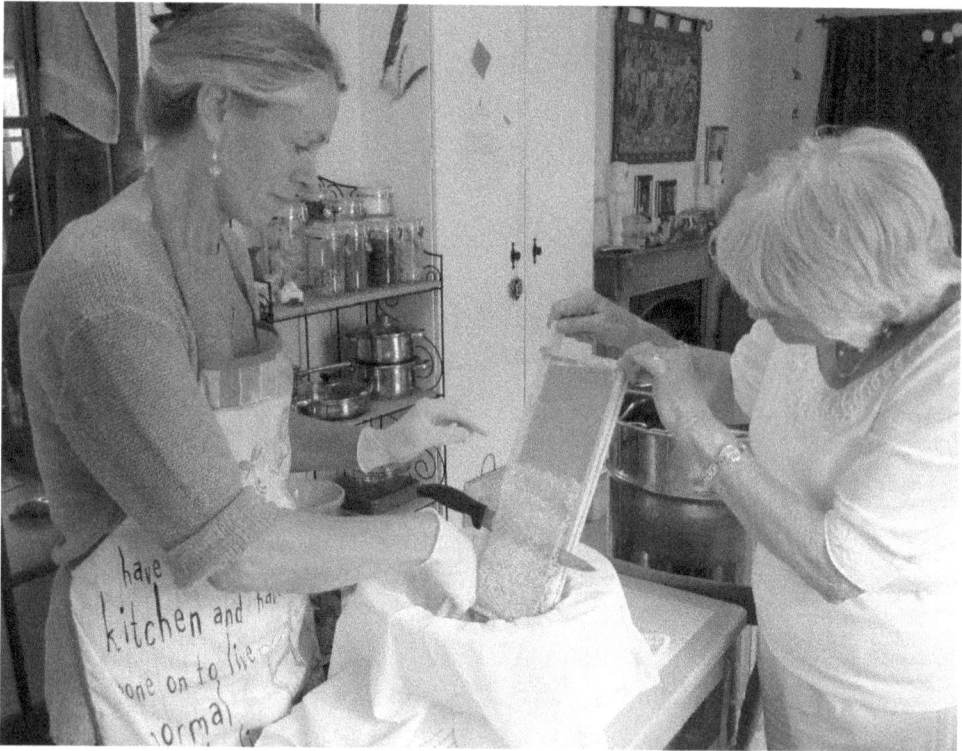

It took a while to get the wax out of the way, but it cut really easily. When both sides of the frame were done, it went into the extractor. My husband couldn't wait any longer and started turning the handle, and the centrafugal force made the honey fly! While he was having fun doing that, Mum and I gathered up the corners of the nylon straining cloth and squeezed the ball of wax inside - as you would if you were making cheese - and the honey just poured out, over my fingers and into the bowl below.

It must be said at this point that both Mum and I were 'tasting' honey liberally, Mum at one stage stood at the sink with both hands covered and carefully - and with many appreciative noises - sucked the honey off each finger, one by one. DEEEEEEEEEEEELICIOUS!!!! We were having hysterics. Pure honey high!

One frame in the extractor was easy. Four frames in the extractor were heavy! We all had a go at turning the handle. 120 turns each way and we were done. All five frames were emptied (although there still seemed to be quite a lot of honey glistening on them) and we were exhausted.

Then the moment of truth. I loosened the wing-nut on the opening at the bottom of the extractor and held a sieve and bucket underneath. The honey just POURED! It was amazing. Little pieces of wax (and the occasional bee leg!) gathered in the sieve. Near the end my husband lifted the extractor and tipped it so that the last of the honey could run easily out of the hole. Finally, all the honey was out.

I put the lid on the bucket and started the slow and arduous process of cleaning up. Honey was everywhere, but it wasn't as bad as it could have been. Any drops on the floor had been cleaned up immediately, so we hadn't walked honey around. It was mostly just the equipment we'd used.

I took the emptied frames back to the hive and gave them back to the bees. There was lots of excitement. Later on, when I went to check, a couple of bees were staggering around outside the hive and I think they might have over-indulged! That night, of course, I wondered if I should have done that, given the frames back to the bees straight away, but my Beekeeping for Dummies book said that the super could be returned directly to them after the honey harvest, so I reckon I did the right thing.

That evening, I stood looking at the honey in the bucket, superimposing on the honey a picture of my bees at work in their hive. I felt quite overcome with emotion. Just gratitude. Enormous gratitude.

Thank you, my bees.

To some people, keeping bees is solely about this –

Add a touch of whimsy, and you end up with this –

All of which is deeply satisfying, but my journey with bees has been about so much more than honey, hasn't it?

1.8.10

I got so wrapped up in the honey harvest I forgot to set down two entries, things which occurred before I took the frames from the hive.

Firstly and most simply, I took a peek into Hive 2, just to make sure all was well. I could see straight away that they needed more space – there were bees on both sides of the crown board and all over the frames in the brood chamber. (I have since attended to this and given them a brand new super with as yet only 8 frames. I've also put in the queen excluder.) Queenie has laid magnificently in the newly drawn cells in the brood chamber, wall-to-wall brood, all sealed, on two frames. A third frame had larvae and eggs, and a fourth had <u>tiny</u> eggs which must have been freshly laid.

All in all it was a calm and quiet hive inspection. One of those where the bees carried on almost as if I wasn't there. So quiet I almost wondered if <u>I</u> was there. I mean, how can it be possible for a human to intrude into the precious inner sanctum of a hive and create barely a ripple? I worked slowly and carefully, giving the bees time to get out of the way of my fingers, and it was wonderful.

I didn't see the queen but there was so much evidence of her presence – her recent presence - I wasn't worried.

Oh, and as an aside, for the second time I saw the single Italian worker in Hive 2. She does stand out so!

Secondly, in the morning before I removed the honey frames, I watched fascinated as a bumble bee wandered along the landing board and made its way <u>into</u> Hive 1! A guard bee tried very hard (but very politely) to make the bumble bee leave, but it was most determined. At one stage a guard bee tried pulling it out of the hive by its fur! I couldn't believe it. But the bumble bee was too big, too strong, and too set on its course. It wandered in regardless.

Very quickly there was a marked change in the hum from the hive, as the word spread. A giant interloper! I watched for a while longer (there was a brief reappearance of the bumble bee's rear end before it disappeared again) but the bumble bee did not come out. I saw no sign of it the next morning. Whether it was still inside (alive? dead?) or whether they had persuaded it to leave, I couldn't tell.

But how bizarre!

> Two days later I found a dead bumble bee on the ground near the hive. Its wings were torn, as if a dozen bees had set upon it and made sure it would never fly again. I couldn't tell if it had been killed by a sting, or whether they had simply held it hostage and it had starved or died of thirst. Either way, my girls had dealt with the threat in a most efficient manner.
>
> I realised, of course, that I could have saved my bees all that bother simply by diverting the bumble bee from its course towards the hive entrance. A mere flick of my finger would have removed the giant from the slate landing board. However, my curiosity got the better of me. I really, <u>really</u> wanted to see how my bees handled it.

3.8.10

I'm nearing the end now of my first year of beekeeping. What an adventure! A few low points, a few moments of concern or confusion, but mostly it's been highs all the way.

I have visited my bees every single day, no matter what the weather. I have watched them, thought about them, and dreamed about them. My bees have kept me awake at night almost more than anything else. The joy they have given me has been amazing. I have loved every minute.

Except being stung, of course. No one could love a bee at that moment. It hurts a lot!

Today my son came rushing into the kitchen to say "Mum, I think your bees are fighting!" and I ran to the apiary to see. In a blink I was smiling and walking back indoors. It was an orientation flight, nothing more. And I realised then how much I have learned. Once I would have stood and watched my bees and wondered what on earth they were up to. Today I could glance at them and in an instant recognise and understand what they were doing.

Thank you, my children-of-the-sun, for everything you have taught me. I'm looking forward to many more happy years of beekeeping ... with your children, of course! And your children's children ......

NOTES

www.ingramcontent.com/pod-product-compliance
Lightning Source LLC
Chambersburg PA
CBHW080055280326

41934CB00014B/3324